Outer Limits

Beyond Thinking

DAVE LEWIS

authorHOUSE®

AuthorHouse™
1663 Liberty Drive
Bloomington, IN 47403
www.authorhouse.com
Phone: 1 (800) 839-8640

Published by AuthorHouse 05/25/2017

ISBN: 978-1-5246-9436-4 (sc)
ISBN: 978-1-5246-9435-7 (e)

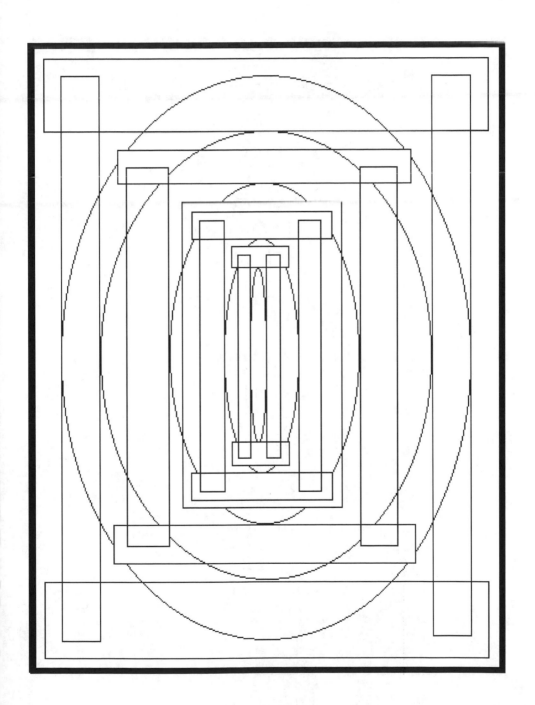

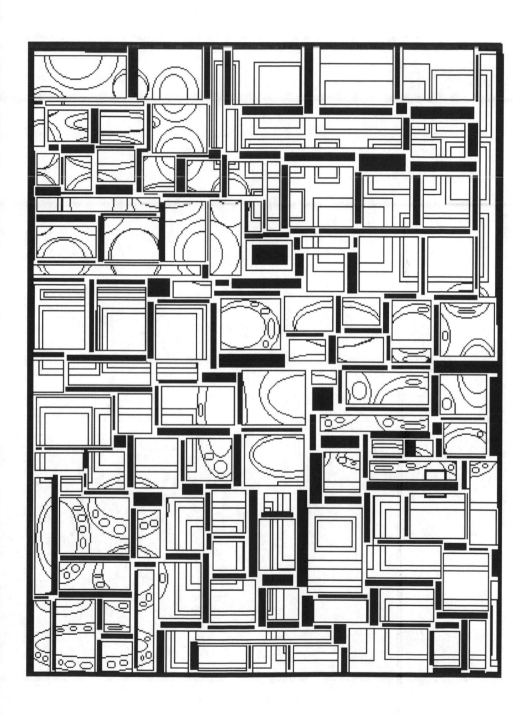

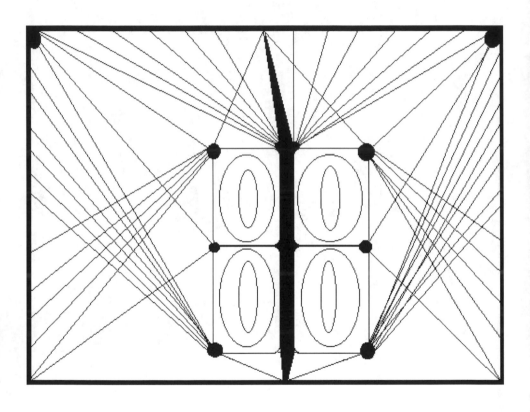

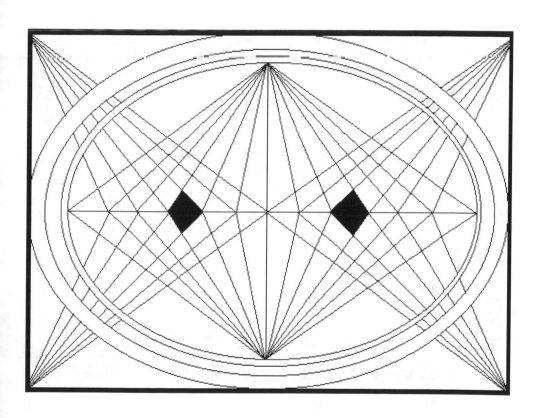

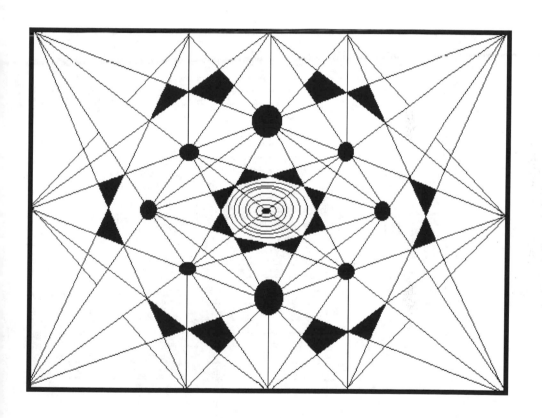

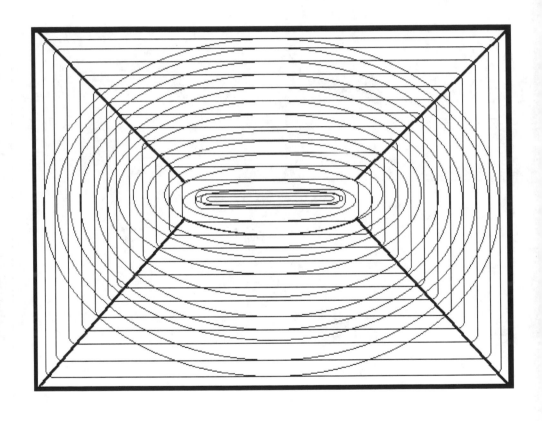

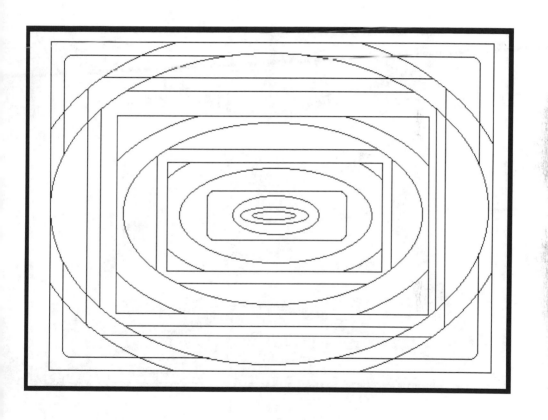

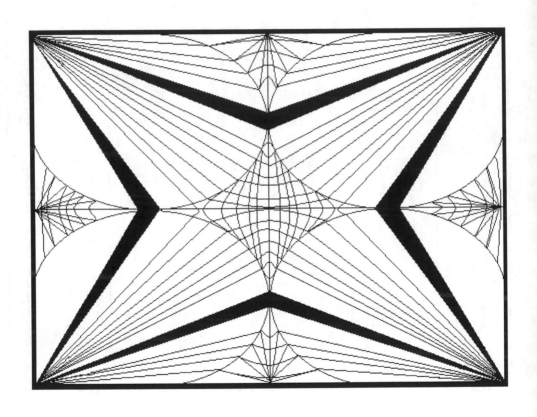

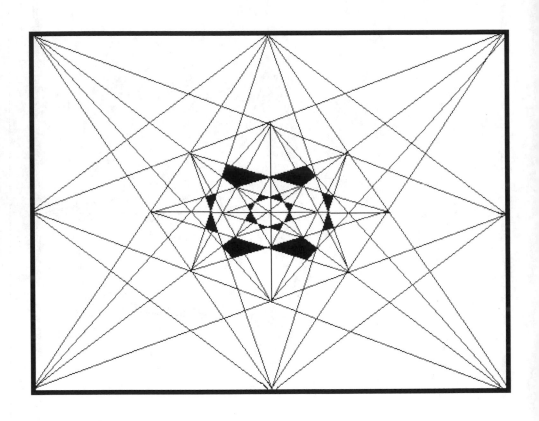

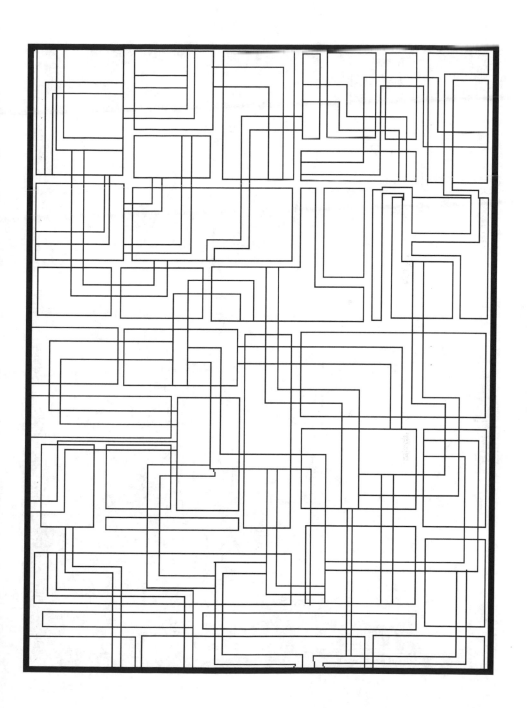

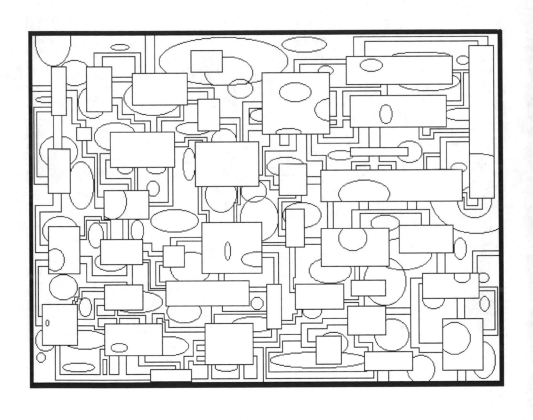

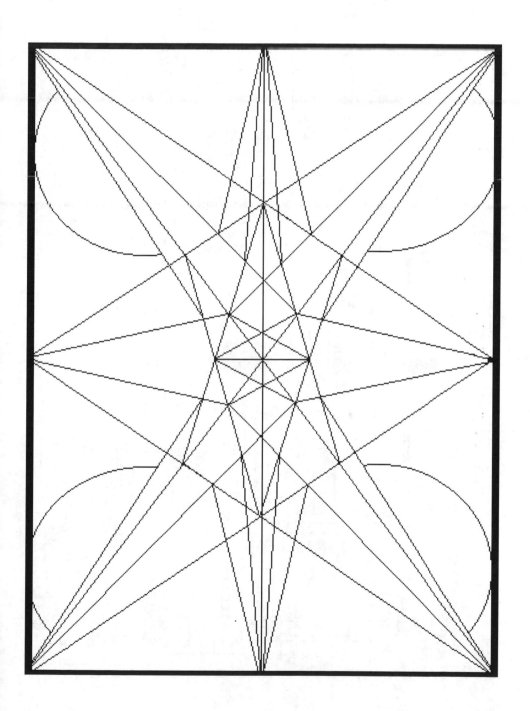

Printed in the United States
By Bookmasters